RELATIONSHIP REPAIR

MANUAL

HOW TO RECONNECT WITH YOUR BELOVED

Lynne Campbell-Gillies
D. Litt et Phil (Psych) (UJ);
Counselling Psychologist

DEDICATION

To my wonderful clients who, in opening up to their unique healing journeys, continue to remind me why I love the work I do. You affirm my belief in the indefatigable human spirit!

To my parents and family: thank you for encouraging and supporting my career. I would like to particularly acknowledge my parents who have been a beacon of light for what it means to have a deeply connected, life-long relationship – not perfect, but always showing up and committed to their special partnership.

To my friends and colleagues who persuaded me to put 'pen to paper' or rather 'fingers on computer keyboard' and get this information down and shared with others, thank you for your encouragement.

Thank you to my good friend Michael Maxwell for your endearing illustrations.

Last but not least, a massive thank you to Sally Shaw for your patience and great editing which brought these words and concepts to life.

ABOUT THE AUTHOR

Dr Lynne Campbell-Gillies (D. Litt et Phil Psychology) has been in private practice for 14 years working with a wide range of adult individuals and couples.

In addition to an improved understanding of their personal issues, Lynne finds that most clients request practical tools to better enjoy their relationships. This is particularly important during times of high stress. She has worked successfully with hundreds of couples and shares in this book several helpful tools and perspectives. Lynne describes herself as a perpetual student of life, pragmatic, balanced and a firm believer in the indefatigable human spirit!

Dr Lynne Campbell-Gillies
Relationship Counselling
Durban
+27 31 764 4886
www.psychealth.co.za

Table of Contents

Introduction

"I just want to be happy."

"I just can't seem to connect with her... What's changed?"

"He's so withdrawn and then he gets short-tempered... I've had enough!"

"We have everything going for us but we fight over the smallest, stupidest things."

"Where is the woman I fell in love with?"

Do you recognise any of these sentiments? You're not alone. This is all standard fare in the world of relationships, all the usual suspects collectively but singularly unique and painful to the individual. If you're in a relationship, then you're in what Elizabeth Kuebler Ross once described as "the tumble-dryer of life".

Relationships are about us, our partners and living life to the fullest. All of it. Intimate relationships are at once glorious, exciting, happy and —equally— challenging, infuriating and perplexing. In-between the loads there are times of peace and contentment. Then life happens and we're thrown back into the tumble-dryer of uncertainty, unfulfilled needs and expectations.

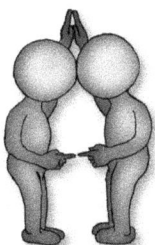

Many of us feel that we should be able to fix something that's not working and that asking for help is a sign of weakness or admitting we may have failed. Ironically, it is often just the little snag that needs pulling to get the pattern back on track. I believe asking for help means we are invested in our relationship and that we value our happiness. At some point all of us need a more objective perspective about our relationship and to avail ourselves of useful tools that will help us reconnect with our partners.

In this case, whether you're in counselling or considering it, or would like a 'top-up' of ideas, this book will be a useful addition to your relationship skill set. It's practical, easy-to-read, has useful exercises to sharpen up or help deepen your knowledge of yourself and how you relate. I invite you to dive in and enjoy the rewarding experience of reconnecting with your beloved.

Ideally, *Relationship Repair Manual* is designed to be worked through as a couple. However, it may very well be that one partner is not ready to do this work. In this case, it would be very helpful for the other to work though it independently to gain insight into themselves and the relationship and be in a position to assist the other in moving forward.

WHY THIS BOOK?

I've worked with hundreds of couples over the years. I have sifted out the best in practical concepts and exercises which have helped many couples re-evaluate and improve their relationships. *Relationship Repair Manual* provides a highly practical, hands-on approach to the most common areas of relationship struggle, in an easy-to-read and handy format. It can be used as a study guide for couples to systematically work through over a couple of months or used specifically to address the challenge currently being experienced in the relationship.

If you can relate to the common experience of a 'disconnected' relationship, then this book is going to help you. You will discover more effective ways to connect with your partner and enjoy the fulfilling and loving relationship you signed up for.

In addition, for those who want a more philosophical look at certain aspects of relationships, you will find at the end of each chapter a section entitled Going Deeper, which delves into the more nuanced or deeper aspects of relationships.

Ultimately, my hope is that you will find this book a useful resource for typical sticking points that many of us encounter in intimate relationships.

Relationships are about connecting. Lynne McTaggart (The Bond, 2011) refers to the "essential impulse of all life", that is, "the will to connect". This is a basic human drive — as basic as eating, drinking and having sex. We know at some intrinsic level that if we are to survive and thrive we need to be able to connect effectively. We cannot NOT relate, so how we relate or seek connection with each other within an intimate relationship is what this book explores.

STRUCTURE OF THE BOOK

I use the metaphor of a 'house' to describe a relationship. This is not a new concept. To me, a house symbolises a body, or structure, which houses you physically, mentally, emotionally and spiritually.

All human beings and most animals, too, create a structure in which they can sleep, rest, procreate, feed and protect themselves and their family. This structure is a 'safe place'. In some ways, it reminds us of the womb — a place where every physical and emotional need was taken care of while we grew and prepared ourselves for life in the outside world. So, it's not a far stretch of the imagination to see that when two people get together, there is an underlying desire to recreate the experience of feeling complete, nurtured and safe. To feel physically and emotionally safe in a loving and connected relationship is a primary goal for all of us. The objective of this book is to help you achieve this goal and the symbolic 'relationship house' is our guiding metaphor for this process.

THE RELATIONSHIP HOUSE

ROOF: EmotionalSecurity
OUTER WALLS: Commitment
INNER WALLS: Boundaries
WINDOWS: Transparency / Honesty
DOOR: Clear Communication
FLOOR: Values; Purpose of the relationship

To take the 'house' metaphor further, at various stages relationships need 'maintenance' and occasional 'repairs'. For example, when a couple have children, or if there is a health or financial crisis, new approaches are required to deal with what is often unchartered territory of life experience. Sometimes, one just needs to change the light-bulb. Other times, a refreshing renovation is indicated.

> A relationship is like a house.
> When a lightbulb burns out
> you do not go and buy a new
> house, you fix the lightbulb.
> -Anonymous

Each chapter deals with a specific relationship area of concern, so the focus of each area will be associated with parts of the relationship house. For example, communication issues will relate to the door, walls to commitment, windows to honesty, etc. While aspects of relationship difficulties are described separately, each aspect depends on and needs to be seen within the context of the entire relationship.

THE IMPORTANCE OF SPACE

Another way a house can be described is in terms of the space it contains. We all need space where we can retreat for quietness and solitude, and there are other types of space, for example where we gather to socialise and share. Space is not just a physical area, but also a psychological-emotional concept. Sometimes a partner will ask 'for space' while they unpack an overwhelming situation, implying the need to get a better perspective or clarity without feeling pressurised. The spaces within your relationship house can sometimes resemble a war-zone, instead of a place of refuge. So, it is my sincerest wish for you, dear reader, to become mindful of the importance of the physical and emotional spaces you create for these impact on the quality of your home and the heart of your relationship.

EXERCISES

You are encouraged to work through the exercises provided at the end of each chapter. They will help clarify your understanding of areas of concern, allowing you to make any relevant changes to your relationship. Work through the exercises alone or with your partner and consider journalling the experience to explore what comes up more deeply. For those who would enjoy some more creative stimulation, do a 'vision board' of your intended relationship. Use photos, images from magazines, drawings, creative writing and so on, on a large piece of paper. You can develop your vision board as you work through the book, or once you've completed it. I have used this concept to plan travel, work, family and relationship intentions using a digital vision board app called MakeAVisionBoard.com.

BASELINE HEALTH CHECK

Before you go any further let's do a health check by rating how satisfied you are with the state of your relationship on a scale of 0 -10, where zero is bad, and 10 is perfect. Consider various aspects of your relationship:

* Are you able to be open and honest in your communications;
* Do you enjoy a good sex-life ("good" is relative, of course, and it's how you perceive this);
* Do you feel emotionally safe to be yourself and are you well-supported by your partner;
* Do you enjoy quality time together such as date nights, holidays, walks or simply a bit of 'down

time' where you sit together enjoying the sunset on your patio;
* Do you openly share your decision-making in various areas such as family, parenting, finance, holidays; and,
* Are you able to effectively resolve conflicts within a short space of time?

There may be other important areas in your relationship that should be factored in, so add these together and find an average score for your current total relationship satisfaction. I suggest you do this assessment individually and then see where you differ with your partner.

At the end of the book and having worked through all the exercises, do another health check. You will hopefully see a substantial improvement in the overall health of your relationship.

DISCLAIMER

You will learn many useful skills and techniques that have helped hundreds of clients, but these exercises do not substitute for therapy where this might be indicated. Resources are listed at the end of the book. Please consult your local directories for appropriate help should you require it. Also note that couples are described as typically male and female but the material is suited to individuals of any gender and sexual orientation.

Chapter 1

WHAT CAUSES COUPLES TO DISCONNECT

There are numerous reasons that a couple begin to disengage with each other. For example, your partner may not be around physically as much due to working long hours, travel, study or commitment to sports goals. Your partner may be around but not present emotionally or mentally due to a debilitating problem they are struggling with. They may be hiding something important they don't feel able to share with you.

Conversely, you may be struggling with an issue you are ashamed of or angry about but don't know how to tell your partner. One of you may be sick. You may have a sick child causing emotional and/or financial strain.

There are any number of reasons that can be identified but underpinning these causes of disengagement is a feeling that it is not safe to discuss the issues for fear of anger or rejection or burdening your partner.

An accumulation of these seemingly weighty concerns when not properly addressed inevitably cause cracks in the relationship. Many couples try to put on a brave face or book a weekend away together, but simply plastering over the cracks hoping the problem will go away will not necessarily resolve the problem.

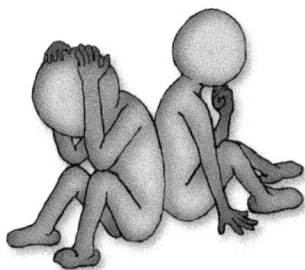

WHAT DOES DISCONNECTION LOOK LIKE?

When we withdraw emotionally and physically, we disconnect from each other, leading to crossed signals or missed cues and less warmth and receptivity. Communication may sputter and start and grow increasingly superficial. One partner may turn away from a kiss or embrace, hurting the other. Then, neither will be willing to sit together on the couch and soon handholding and affection disappears, even outside the home in cheerful company.

For many couples, this signals barriers to intimacy and they withdraw sexually as well. Emotional hurt tends to go hand-in-hand with physical rejection. While many couples begin therapy by saying they have communication problems, often it doesn't take long before the discussion circles to sex, or indeed, the lack of it for at least one of the partners. Satisfying sex is communication and connection on a profoundly instinctual and spiritual level.

Sex is an intrinsic expectation for most couples, it is also a cause of huge emotional vulnerability, particularly when your partner avoids contact with you. When a couple is emotionally disconnected, both feel disempowered by the situation. In some cases, sex may be used as a 'weapon of war' by some in the belief that they can take 'revenge' for their hurt by withholding sex.

For others, the hurt is so deep that it has nothing to do with taking revenge. Rather it is a shutting down and protection of their emotional and physical vulnerability. Withdrawal of intimate affection is felt as rejection and often interpreted as betrayal. This fuels the feeling of disconnection even further.

Take the case of Sally and Geoff. A couple in their mid-40s, Sally is a Sales Executive in a medium-sized car retail operation. Geoff is head of IT at a bank's headquarters in the city. They have two children—Peter, 12, and Lizzie, 14. They have been married for 16 years, but first met soon after they had left school. Sally called for the appointment. Frustration and exhaustion came through in her voice when she asked for my first available appointment.

FIRST SESSION

Sally: "I'm tired of asking Geoff to help more around the house, to get his head out of the laptop in the evenings... he's been staring at screens all day at work, why does he need to do it for hours at home too?"

Sally's voice was growing highly pitched and tears were beginning to well in her eyes.

Geoff looked at her glumly, and at me with a face that said, "I don't know what more I can do. I just can't win." Geoff looked completely defeated and close to surrendering to whatever fate lay before him.

This was a couple in a state of 'disconnect'. Channels of normal and fulfilling communication appeared to be closed. Sally barked instructions to Geoff and the kids while she was rushing out the door for work, and Geoff mumbled his acknowledgement of tasks to do. This couple were like the proverbial 'ships passing in the night'.

One of the primary reasons for a disconnected relationship is a feeling that it is not safe to talk about something. If you feel momentarily criticised or rebuffed by your partner — "Are you serious, Sally? You want me to fetch the kids AND do a full day's work?" — and you're able to talk about the way the issue was handled or comfortably choose to ignore it, then the chances of recovering from the put-down are strong.

Conversely, if you experience hurtful behaviour frequently (such as being criticised, put down or demeaned) then it is highly likely that neither of you feels emotionally safe enough to discuss a problem. To cope with this, you may react in an equally critical, aggressive or avoidant way, because you've probably tried to talk about the problem, but your partner seems not to hear you. This is the slippery slide to a disconnected relationship and as discussed, sexual issues are often experienced.

An interesting perspective on why couples disconnect is found in Patricia Love and Steven Stosny's book: *Why Women Talk and Men Walk, 2010*. They describe the man's biological and neurological hardwiring as the provider/protector, and the woman's hardwiring' as the tender/befriender. When a man senses that he is not able to or is prevented from doing his 'job' of providing and protecting, a deep-seated unconscious-feeling of shame is triggered. He tends to manifest his feelings of inadequacy or shame by behaving aggressively or withdrawing and retreating.

When a woman feels she is not able to do her 'job' of tending and befriending, she feels alienated and this can manifest in the form of anxiety.

She (hurt): "You're not listening to me, Bob! You're more interested in what's happening on your phone than in me..."

He (aggressively): "Stop nagging, me. When I tell you what I think you should do you ignore what I've suggested anyway."

Love and Stosny's book presents a gender stereotype towards the male in the role of provider/protector and the female tender-befriender, however it's understood that these roles could be reversed. The underlying message is that when a couple feels emotionally unsafe to constructively communicate their feelings for fear of being criticised, dismissed or ignored, it shuts the relationship down. They give up trying to emotionally connect with each other.

By learning to recognise patterns of disconnection and adopting the practical communication methods you will learn in this book, you will feel and behave in an emotionally safe way with your partner, regain each other's trust and achieve a feeling of true connection.

When I explained the concept of provider/protector and tender/befriender roles and how couples that don't validate each other begin to feel disconnected from each other, Sally and Geoff immediately relate to the scenario. They understand that Geoff has withdrawn from the relationship because he feels criticised and incapable of living up to Sally's expectations.

At the same time, Sally can't find the words or any other way to convey her frustration with Geoff for his apparent lack of involvement in the marriage. Her disappointment and fear regarding the state of their relationship is evident to Geoff, but because he feels incapable of meeting his perception of Sally's requirements, his shame and embarrassment causes him to retreat into a protective shell. Neither feels heard by the other.

Both feel emotionally unsafe to be themselves and the relationship is temporarily paralysed. So where to from here?

Chapter 2

A SOLID FOUNDATION:

VALUES AND PURPOSE OF RELATIONSHIP

To begin the process of building a house, one needs a floorplan. Usually the floorplan outlines details of the foundation. We know that a well-constructed, solid foundation — the floor — is essential to the stability of a house. And so it is with a relationship.

The foundation of a relationship may be viewed as the purpose of the relationship as well as a conscious and intact set of personal and relationship values. In addition to knowing your own values, knowing your partner's values, history, hopes, dreams, worries and joys helps provide a strong, confident basis for your relationship.

VALUES

Do you know what your top five personal values are? Do you know your partner's top values?

There are times when we experience life as stressful or overwhelming, and when we analyse these situations we find that they are out of alignment with our inherent value system. Becoming aware of what is important in the way we live and work (our values) helps us to better manage a multitude of life situations.

Human behaviour expert and author Dr John Demartini reminds us: "No person is committed to anything but the fulfilment of their own highest values." In other words, the areas of life where we spend the most time and effort, where we feel the most energised and connected, illustrates where and what we most highly value.

Values tend to be stable over time, but some may change according to circumstances. For example, a mother with young children will probably value free time a lot more today than before she had children. The following exercise helps establish your current top personal values.

VALUES EXERCISE

I suggest both parties spend five to 10 minutes (separately) working out their values, and when the exercise is complete, discuss the results with each other.

Read through the sheet of core values below and identify at least 10 that you strongly resonate with. Please add any values that you believe are missing from the list. Think carefully whether the selected values describe how you live your life at present.

Achievement	Integrity
Time freedom	Adventure
Intellectual status	Truth
Affection	Leadership
Wealth	Arts
Location	Wisdom
Change and Variety	Loyalty
Working with others	Community
Meaningful work	Working alone
Cooperation	Merit
Competition	Money
Creaitivity	Nature
Efficiency	Order and Stability
Ethical practice	Personal development
Excellence	Freedom
Excitement	Physical challenge
Fame	Pleasure
Financial gain	Power and Authority

Friendships	Privacy
Family	Quality relationships
Growth	Recognition
Health	Responsibility and
Helping others	Accountability
Honesty	
Independence	

— C. Roberts: Fifth Discipline Fieldbook

After you've selected 10 items, eliminate five of these. The remaining five will be your top five values.

SCORE YOUR VALUES

Next, score each of your top five values out of 10, where 10 is the belief that your value is perfectly fulfilled.

It's possible that one or two of your values are not being lived out to their full potential. This is an opportunity for you to set some goals to increase the scores over a specified time, if possible.

If family is one of your top five values, rate how fulfilled you feel with regard to this value. If the score is less than 7/10 set some goals to help increase this score. For example: spend more quality time with my kids (specify what, when, how?). If you're keeping a journal you can revert to the score in a few months' time and see if it has improved.

Share your top five values and scores of each value with your partner.

How many values are the same or similar to your partner's values? Were you aware of your partner's values and scores?

In summary, living in alignment with your values reduces stress. When both people in the relationship know each other's personal values they can help support them. This is a key factor in a healthy relationship.

Knowing and following your personal set of values forms the ground upon which you sustain a positive and connected relationship. This process will also assist you when you feel your boundaries have been challenged. More about boundaries later.

MISSION STATEMENT

Having identified your values, the next step to ensure you have a solid foundation is becoming clear about the purpose of your relationship.

I frequently ask couples to imagine their relationship is like a business. Assume you are the owners of this 'business'. A crucial element of running a business involves strategising and setting goals, and, to do this effectively, one develops a mission statement. This generally includes the business's purpose: to make a profit doing something you enjoy; core values: to adhere to ethical business practices; and setting goals: ensuring customer satisfaction and employee wellbeing.

Similarly with your relationship. The purpose of your relationship is like the 'big picture' or the blue-print of why you're together. In developing your mission statement, you will consider what it is that brought you together and what keeps you together. In addition, you will include some or all of the values you both have. For example: "We are a couple who love and respect each other, have many common interests and two beautiful children. We have endured some hardships which have made us stronger and we are completely committed to our journey together…"

Once you have the big picture, set down some goals that you know will help achieve and sustain this picture. For example: "We plan an annual family holiday; as a couple we set up at least four brief getaways a year…"

EXERCISE: DEVELOP YOUR RELATIONSHIP MISSION STATEMENT

For example: "Our relationship is founded upon our love and respect for each other, our belief in the sanctity of our marriage vows and the care and nurturing of our children. We aim to commit to this mission statement by checking in with each other on a weekly basis when, as a couple, we will enjoy at least an hour of quality time reconnecting on whatever level is appropriate (mental, physical, emotional), evaluating where we're at and adjusting plans going forward if necessary."

Most couples become completely invested in the process and will laminate the completed mission statement and place it in a strategic place (dressing room mirror, for example) where they can see it daily.

As time goes on and circumstances change, the

mission statement will need to be adjusted. In the meantime, enjoy the process and have fun reconnecting with your dreams and aspirations.

Going Deeper

Here are the values I stand for: honesty, equality, kindness, compassion, treating people the way you want to be treated and helping those in need. To me, those are traditional values.
— Ellen DeGeneres

JOURNALLING MY VALUES AND EXPLORING MY GOALS

I have learned over time that being conscious of my personal values allows me to live in alignment with my personal goals, as well as keep me focused on my life's purpose. I have a strong empathic streak, caring deeply about people, but also for all life and its creatures. I also love travelling as this fuels my value of learning about life in general, and about people and human behaviour in particular. I read extensively. My life's purpose is to help others and in doing so inspire and be inspired by those I come into contact with. This is what makes me feel well and connected with life.

Life's not all rosy and perfection, of course. I can report some dismal failures, but rather let me tell you how I deal with life's inevitable setbacks. I contact my valuable support base (a small group of close friends) to talk through what's bothering me. I know I can rely on this group of friends for honest yet compassionate feedback. I may meditate or listen to music or go to the gym for 30 minutes, or a combination of these. It doesn't usually take too long to re-align my values and purpose in life now with an added dimension of personal awareness.

Chapter 3

THE DOOR: EFFECTIVE COMMUNICATION

If you've had the experience in your relationship where you've thought, "if only we could communicate better" then you're not alone. It's true, the most frequent reason that couples seek counselling tends to be around 'communication issues', which of itself is a good sign since opening up avenues of communication is like throwing the door open to let in fresh air and light.

There are many reasons that couples experience communication difficulties so let's get a handle on the door to gain a broad understanding of the subject.

STYLES OF COMMUNICATION

Imagine that before verbally or non-verbally expressing yourself, information goes through two primary filters: **thinking** and **feeling**. Consider that both you and your partner's entire life experience, personality and understanding of the world, as well as present mood and circumstance, are filtered and projected via your unique thoughts and feelings to the outer world. It's hardly surprising that what is finally verbalised is sometimes 'lost in translation'. Communication is not only hearing what comes out of your partner's mouth, but reading and interpreting all the non-verbal cues and signals that are given off. Striving for clarity about what each other is saying is a vital component of communication.

DIFFERENT 'VOICES' IN COMMUNICATION

With the filtering process in mind, and with the intention of more skilled communication, I'd like to share with you a simplified version of Eric Berne's Transactional Analysis where you will learn a technique of communicating from the so-called Adult Voice. For more detail on this please refer to *Lessons for The Adult Child* by Judy Klipin (2010).

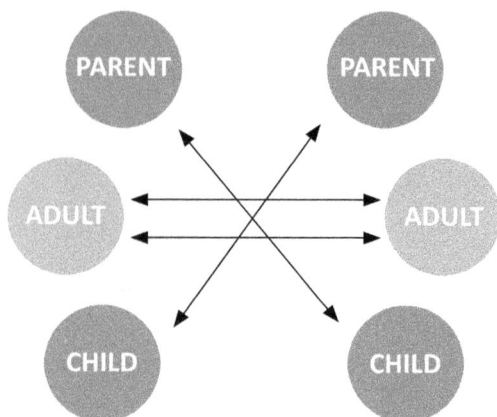

The **Parent** voice is critical ("how many times must I tell you to put the cap on the toothpaste?") or nurturing ("I'm telling you this for your own good... you really need a haircut"). The characteristic of these parental voices is that we use them to talk at our partner, rather than with our partner; there is a quality of talking down to the other. The reaction of someone receiving this parental style of communication is typically one of a disempowered **Child**.

Let's return to the case of Sally and Geoff. During our first session, in answer to how each of them described their perceptions of the relationship, Sally said: "I'm so tired of talking to the back of your head, Geoff. Your primary attention is clearly what's on your laptop." This is an example of Sally talking down to Geoff. She uses the Critical Parent voice with the consequence that Geoff would feel like an admonished Child.

The Child voice is a deeply embedded reactive voice. It is a defensive response learned during childhood in interaction with the parent. Most of us will have grown up with parental injunctions such as "Don't do that again!"which we learned to deflect or absorb in the form of a rebellious "I will if I want!" or a compliant "Yes, OK... I'm sorry... ", or a nonchalant response "Whatever...".

The person responding from a Child position feels disrespected and simultaneously disempowered. Recall when your partner criticised you for something, justified or not. How did it feel? Unfair? When someone speaks to you in a Parental way you will typically respond in a Child voice. If you speak to your partner from a disempowered, defensive or avoidant Child voice, your partner will react from a Parental voice. The outcome of Parent-Child styles of communication is a feeling of lose-lose, for both parties.

In response to Sally's criticism of Geoff spending time buried in his laptop and, with the clear insinuation from Sally that Geoff preferred his own company to that of hers, Geoff responded: "I just can't seem to please you, and I'm so tired of your nagging." Geoff responds from a place of disempowerment. He sounds angry and defeated.

Both Sally and Geoff feel paralysed by the state of their relationship. Neither of them seem to have the wherewithal to remedy the situation because they both feel hurt. Their feelings of hurt and betrayal have reached a point where they feel they can't communicate openly without the threat of being criticised or judged. The couple have become emotionally disconnected.

Couples who feel emotionally disconnected have generally slipped into a Parent-Child style of communicating. If you relate to this experience, you are in a power-struggle trying to assert your needs and no one is listening. You act out from an authoritative, bossy Parent position, or you act out from a defensive Child position. Both positions leave you feeling emotionally drained.

How do we overcome this lose-lose style of communication?

We move in to what's called the **Adult** voice. Looking at the diagram, one sees that the communication dynamic is immediately different. Firstly, it's assumed that a couple is communicating on an equal level so there is not an unequal, top-down style of communication. From here, other logical assumptions can be made, for example, they are not in a combative, power-driven position; they treat each other as equals and they assume a collaborative attitude.

SPEAKING FROM THE ADULT VOICE

Here are some key points about communicating with an Adult voice.

* The objective of Adult-Adult communication is to find common ground, possibly with some compromises, and arrive at a solution where both parties feel heard and appreciated.

* Communication is underpinned by an attitude of respect. Respect for ourself and our partner (refer to your Values in Chapter 1, and to Chapter 5).

* We engage with our partners as equals, consciously using skills such as looking at each other whilst talking (as opposed to being distracted by the TV or our phones).

* We listen carefully with a view to understanding, rather than waiting to put our own view across.

* We clarify the information, exchanging and building on ideas and information.

* There is minimal emotion. When we are angry or sad, we are unlikely to rationally discuss and resolve a matter. Emotions often sabotage rational thinking. If you are feeling emotional, consider taking a walk or distracting yourself for a short while, and together with your partner, agree to resume your conversation at a specific time a bit later.

* Significantly, it puts the issue and not the couple at the centre of negotiation.

In summary, the attitude of an Adult-Adult style of communication is one of co-operation and respect, not of demand or defence. You do not avoid having the conversation, as you know the issue is likely to fester causing you to cycle back to the Parent-Child style of communication. The Adult-Adult conversation reveals a couple committed to finding a win-win solution.

WHAT LANGUAGE DO YOU USE?

In addition to the way we talk with each other, sometimes we also need to check on the language we use. We take for granted that just because we both speak the same language, in this case English, we expect to be perfectly understood.

However, as we mature into our relationship and expect to be automatically understood, sometimes our partner completely misunderstands us. Gary Chapman describes a way around this common problem in his book *Five Languages of Love*.

Communicating and connecting effectively with your mate means that you are aware of not only your own tone of voice, the attitude with which you convey information, but knowing and using your partner's specific love language. Here are the basic love languages, according to Chapman:

* Words of Affirmation: Verbal appreciation or encouragement. "You look great in that suit."

*   Quality Time: Being present, listening; sharing time with each other.

*   Receiving Gifts: Visual symbols of love, not necessarily expensive gifts but meaningful expressions of your love and commitment such as flowers, chocolate, a small article of clothing, etc.

*   Acts of Service: Doing simple chores around the house or running an errand.

*   Physical Touch: In addition to sex, physical expressions of love such as holding hands can also be a meaningful language of love. Asking your partner what she/he prefers in this respect is crucial.

DO YOU KNOW EACH OTHER'S LOVE LANGUAGES?

EXERCISE

Write down what you think are your preferred love language/s. Next, write down what you think are your partner's love language/s, noting how often in the past week you have been on the receiving end of these acts of love. How often have you communicated using your partner's specific love language in the past week?

Do this exercise separately. Then swap your responses with your partner and discuss. It would be useful to journal your insights about communication skills in general. What stands out for you in terms of the concepts discussed in this chapter?

LISTENING

A critical component of good communication is the ability to quietly listen to your partner when he/she talks. If there is one skill that will help enhance your relationship it is the power of listening attentively. Listening attentively, without preparing your 'defence', takes practice. It requires calmness and an open mind.

Good listeners show their attentiveness both verbally and non-verbally. They will face the speaker and assume a posture of openness. They will invite the other's participation in the communication with a few words of encouragement. They will limit the number of questions as this may derail the speaker's train of thought and make the conversation more about the listener. A good listener knows when to be silent.

THE IMPORTANCE OF 'SELF-SOOTHING'

Couples have disagreements and are bound to argue and fight. That's a given. What's not a given is how we pre-empt or recover from conflict situations. If you know your spouse is coming home angry because of a specific situation, you can prepare to meet his anger calmly. Or if, after a difficult talk, you have a favourite biscuit on hand to go with coffee, that shows you have brought forethought and care to the table. It is these situations where we discover that we have communication issues.

Where we have been triggered in an emotional flare-up with our partner, it is useful to employ ways of calming ourselves down. Storming down the passage while muttering under your breath isn't going to help.

The truth is that emotional reactions need to be remedied from the inside, as an individual. It's an awareness that instead of feeling victimised and blaming the other, we rather take control of the situation and own our feelings.

One strategy for reducing emotion in the heat of the moment may be to tell your partner that you need to 'take a breather' so you can return and deal with the sensitive issue more calmly. Then, take a walk outside; or distract yourself with a small task; or simply go to another space in the house and quietly breathe and count to 10. A more sustained approach to lowering your stress levels might be taking regular yoga classes, meditation, gym or other forms of exercise such as cycling or walking in nature. Being in a healthy, connected relationship requires taking responsibility for your own wellbeing too. Find ways to relax and centre yourself so that when you communicate with your beloved, you do so completely and openly with a view to truly hearing your partner and honouring his or her needs.

EXERCISE

Journal your intention to better manage negative stressors and then list goals to achieve this. What are these stressors? Some things are beyond your control, some are not. Specify these. What do you find helps you de-stress?

Honour yourself by taking five to 10 minutes per day to de-stress. Listen to soothing music, have a warm shower, or treat yourself to a guided relaxation meditation such as provided in the following link: [http://media.dartmouth.edu/~healthed/mindfulness_just_this_breath. mp3]. Journal your experience of this exercise and any other insights that come to you regarding the area of communication.

Going Deeper

Between what is said and not
meant and what is meant and
not said, most love is lost
— Khalil Gibran

I love this this quotation because it encapsulates the essence of "communication problems".

Communication is an art and a skill. I see it as an ability which, if applied with awareness and compassion, is heart-fully articulated. In other words, when we articulate a message from a position of integrity (where our head and heart are aligned) we may avoid a place where 'love is lost'.

How often have we blurted out a comment only to regret it immediately afterwards? I know I have. When I reflect on the circumstances, they inevitably point to a lack of care. Either I was stressed, tired or I was simply not paying attention.

A key attitude for all positive human interactions is paying attention. All the techniques and knowledge in the world won't serve or fulfil you if you do not cultivate the ability to pay attention both to yourself and your partner. Paying attention when we are engaging with our partner helps us communicate clearly and respectfully. It helps bridge the occasional difficulty between "what is said and not meant, and what is meant and not said". This is the quality of the Adult style of communication. Not always an easy task, but with the gift of rewarding outcomes to aspire towards.

It's all very well talking about paying attention and communicating with integrity, but what if you're stressed? Most of us feel stressed or simply disengaged from life at various times. If, however, you're finding you're more stressed than normal then it's time to pay attention to yourself.

An obvious sign that you're needing to stop and take stock is when you're irritable or moody. Perhaps you can relate to the words of Gibran above: Are you not saying what you mean? Do you find you're unable to articulate what you feel?

Perhaps one or more of these suggestions will help you reset and re-engage with life:

* Exercise: Physical exercise helps clear the mind as well as physically energise the body.

* Nutrition: What we put in our bodies not only affects us physically but also directly affects the brain and our moods.

* Mental-breather: Take a mini-break, an evening out with your beloved at a favourite restaurant; having some close friends for a meal; a weekend away in the mountains or a day at the beach.

In addition, the value of regular meditation or prayer cannot be underestimated. Any form of activity that helps us become present, such as yoga, tai chi or just stretching, is a gift to our overall wellbeing.

Chapter 4

THE INNER WALLS:

THE IMPORTANCE OF BOUNDARIES

> When we fail to set boundaries
> and hold people accountable,
> we feel used and mistreated.
> — Brené Brown

Trish and Michael set up an appointment to discuss difficulties in their marriage.

Michael, tall with a disarming smile, begins at Trish's prompting by saying: "We have a pretty good marriage. We've got two teenage kids who are doing well at school, and even if I say so myself, are well-adjusted and happy. But there are times when I need to work late. The economy is not good and there are huge stresses at work..."

Trish interrupts: "You're not the only one with stress at work..."

Michael rolls his eyes and continues: "... and so it's unavoidable that I need to keep the engine running. I wish Trish would cut me some slack and understand that I sometimes forget to phone and let her know I'm running late."

"Sometimes! At least three or four times a week!" cries Trish with tears in her eyes.

Trish then stated that because she felt unable to communicate and resolve this issue, she began to fear that Michael may be having an affair. Michael was quick to dispel this "nonsense". This destructive interaction is hurtful and exhausting for everyone and reveals that trust has broken between the two.

Boundaries can be physical, emotional and/or psychological. Boundaries are important for the individual and they're important for the relationship. In a healthy relationship each person has well-defined boundaries based on their sense of self-worth, their values and respect for others.

For example, respecting your partner's privacy certainly means not rifling through her handbag or scrolling through his phone. Establishing boundaries can sometimes be quite daunting, particularly if you believe they've been previously transgressed. However, in a healthy relationship partners will encourage each other to voice their needs or concerns without fear of rejection. A characteristic of a happy, connected and emotionally safe relationship is when a couple understands and accepts each other's boundaries. Healthy boundaries also reveal a trusting relationship.

When you feel your boundaries have been violated, it is imperative to voice this and ensure that the integrity of your boundary is restored. Every relationship will probably experience challenges to its integrity at some point. For example, your partner may post something personal online without your consent. A more extreme violation would be having an affair.

Often, boundary violations are a result of one party simply not paying sufficient attention to their relationship. For example, there may be excessive work commitments or problems with extended family. The violation in such a case, may be an issue of poor communication whereby you or your partner are not able to openly express yourselves about feeling neglected or the overwhelming pressure to perform at work without the fear of being criticised. When you're not able to openly discuss the feeling then you may suppress your hurt, which ends up causing more resentment. Inevitably, the hurt comes through in the form of sarcasm, moodiness or biting remarks. (See *The Four Horsemen of the Apocalypse* in Chapter 5).

Boundary violations are a betrayal of a couple's expectations. In the case of an affair, the hurt experienced by the injured party can be traumatising. The subject of affairs and infidelity is well-documented; it is also a subject that deserves detail that cannot be sufficiently covered in this book. If you are struggling to deal with the fall-out of an affair, please seek the help of a qualified therapist or counsellor. I have also suggested some authors who may assist you in understanding this painful experience at the end of the book.

When individuals are clear about their boundaries, they don't need to resort to passive, aggressive or passive-aggressive behaviour to let their partner know that they are unhappy with the way they have been treated. For example, instead of Trish complaining and tearfully blaming Michael for how she feels, which she is expressing in the Child voice, she might assume a more assertive, and Adult, position by saying: "I understand that you are under a lot of stress at work, but I feel that not letting me know you're running late is inconsiderate. Please phone or message in the future."

The old adage, you teach others how to treat you is very important in all our relationships. It also ensures that your relationship boundaries are valued.

THE DRAMA TRIANGLE

Another useful concept to assist couples when they find themselves in situations where boundaries are muddied and they are unable to resolve a particular situation, is the **Drama Triangle**.

Take the case of John and Patrick. John complains: "I feel like I'm on my own 24/7 supporting this family." Patrick reacts: "How dare you suggest that I don't contribute!" Then, John feels he needs to back down to keep the peace, so after some back-and-forth bickering about who does what, he says, in a conciliatory way, "Okay! I guess I'll have to take over and sort out the finances."

Clearly, the couple have not asserted their boundaries apropos finances and the result is an example of what Stephen Karpman, M.D. describes as the Drama Triangle.

The following illustration is a model of drama-intense social interactions played out constantly, as in the case above.

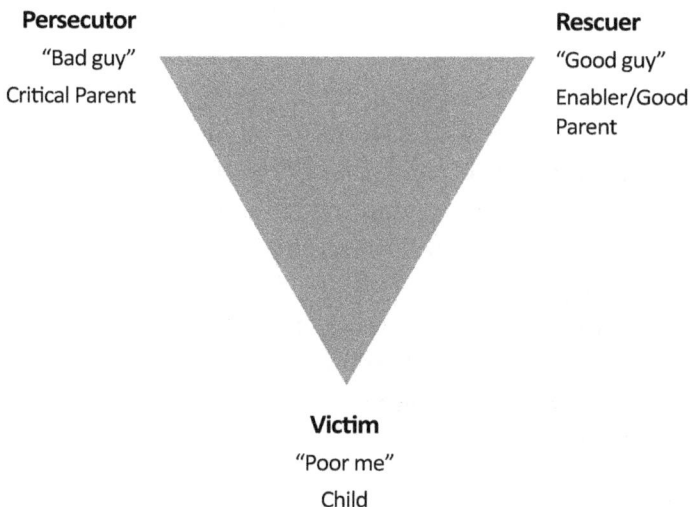

Persecutor
"Bad guy"
Critical Parent

Rescuer
"Good guy"
Enabler/Good Parent

Victim
"Poor me"
Child

Applying the **Drama-triangle** model to John and Patrick, John feels hard done by: "I feel like I'm on my own 24/7 supporting this family", displaying the role of the Victim. John's poor-me message attracts an aggressive, Persecutor, reaction from Patrick: "How dare you suggest that I don't contribute!"

The **Persecutor-Victim** volleying of defend and attack may continue for a while before one of them decides to Rescue the situation out of a sense of guilt or appeasement. In this situation, John became the **Rescuer**: "Okay! I guess I'll have to take over and sort out the finances."

Unfortunately, this does not resolve the problem. The person who has been "Rescued" feels subtly ashamed or denigrated. If Patrick had been part of a negotiation where they had both reached a mutually agreed solution, the outcome would have been more satisfactory. Instead, the Rescuer has perpetuated the "drama" by solving the situation for his partner, instead of with him. Both parties feel dissatisfied because the one feels patronised, and the other resentful.

If this style of communication is regular within a relationship, it suggests co-dependence stemming from unresolved childhood experiences that may require a deep level of therapy. Nonetheless, catching it in the present provides wonderful opportunities for correction.

So, how could John and Patrick have resolved this situation? Here is a basic step-by-step process to leave the drama:

1. Acknowledge that you're in a drama triangle.

2. Once you're aware that you're in this unhelpful cycle of communication, ask yourself which role/s you were playing – Persecutor, Rescuer and/or Victim?

3. Identify how each role felt (I feel sad and misunderstood – I am playing Victim). You have now begun a process of leaving the drama.

4. Take a few minutes of breathing space to lower the emotional level and then, when you're ready, invite your partner to help both of you resolve the issue.

Timing is an essential element in resolving problems. We aren't generally able to make rational decisions when we're highly emotional. Ideally, take a break and return to the 'negotiating table' when you both feel your equilibrium has been re-established.

To lower the emotions, I often suggest to my clients that they take a walk around the garden or sit somewhere quiet and possibly distract themselves with a small task or listen to some music. Taking a few good, deep breaths is also very useful in calming us down. Negotiations can then resume on a more even footing.

Becoming skilled at moving out of the drama triangle means that you are also becoming comfortable with your boundaries. You realise that you are responsible for your wellbeing, and don't need to be a Victim to your circumstances. You also don't have to act out your frustration with a situation by being the Persecutor. Nor do you need to Rescue the other person.

You understand that one of the most effective ways of addressing a problem is to adopt the Adult voice. An Adult voice suggests you are aware of your self-worth and your boundaries are intact. Communication is constructive and straight forward.

John: "Pat, my boss has increased my workload following Lilly's retrenchment last month. Could we chat about how you might help me with the house hold finances?"

Patrick: "Sure, let's talk about it after supper this evening."

While navigating boundaries can be tricky over the course of time in relationships, couples who have clear boundaries also have a good framework to return to should the boundary be crossed.

EXERCISE

Based on your values and mission statement (Chapter 2) discuss with each other what you consider to be your personal and relationship boundaries.

Write down a summary of these. Consider updating your Mission Statement by incorporating these boundaries so they are clearly understood and visible.

Going Deeper

"Your relationship with yourself
sets the tone for every other
relationship you have."
— Anonymous

The Four Agreements

BE IMPECCABLE WITH YOUR WORD

* Speak with integrity
* Say only what you mean
* Avoid using the word to speak against yourself or gossip about others.
* Use the power of your word in the direction of truth and love

DON'T TAKE ANYTHING PERSONALLY

* Nothing others do is because of you
* What others say and do is a projection of their own dream
* When you are immune to the opinions and actions of others, you won't be the victim of needless suffering

DON'T MAKE ASSUMPTIONS

* Find the courage to ask questions and to express what you really want
* Communicate with others as clearly as you can to avoid misunderstandings, sadness and drama
* With just this one agreement you can completely transform your life

ALWAYS DO YOUR BEST

* Your best is going to change from moment to moment: it will be different when you are healthy as opposed to sick
* Under any circumstance, simply do your best and you will avoid self-judgment, self-abuse and regret

These simple agreements outlined by Don Miguel Ruiz in his book *The Four Agreements* are in fact quite profound. For a thorough explanation of each of these personal agreements, I encourage you to read it yourself. In the meantime, consider this summarised version and see how you might apply the wisdom of each agreement to your life.

Personally, I find agreement Number 2 challenging at times. "Don't take anything personally". When tired or stressed, don't you feel less centred and more emotionally vulnerable? This is when another person's inadvertent remarks can quickly trigger a defensive action, and a cycle of attack/defend can unfold, leaving you drained.

However, if you were able to be present during the apparent verbal attack by your partner, you would easily see that the issue, while directed at you, is in fact projected from your partner's feeling of fear or hurt. You would probably engage differently with your partner from this more conscious perspective.

Living your life according to these agreements will certainly help you to find more peace and harmony both in your personal sense of well-being as well as enhance your ability to have clearer boundaries in your relationships. A photocopy of The Four Agreements on the fridge is a great reminder for everyone.

Chapter 5

THE LOAD-BEARING WALLS:

RESPONSIBILITY AND COMMITMENT

If you aren't constructively
contributing to the relationship,
then you are destructively
contaminating it...
— P C McGraw

One of the most important qualities of a healthy, committed relationship is the ability of partners to be emotionally responsible. Being emotionally responsible means that we take responsibility for how we treat ourselves and others relative to emotional safety, happiness and self-worth. The analogy of load-bearing walls speaks to our personal responsibility for ourselves.

A responsible partner is aware that it is not the task of the other to provide for their happiness. By giving your partner the burden of ensuring your happiness you are handing over the responsibility (and the consequences of this) to another. This can only lead to resentment and unhappiness.

Consider the case of John and Patrick in the previous chapter. John says: "I feel like I'm on my own 24/7 supporting this family". We can assume from this statement that John has not been successful in communicating his need for additional support. He has resorted to expressing himself in a Victim or "poor me" way to try to get Patrick's attention. This form of manipulative communication had the opposite effect with Patrick, who reacted angrily. If John had been more assertive, he might have said: "Patrick, I know I have taken responsibility for managing our finances, but certain issues keep cropping up and I would value your input. Can we chat about this?" Expressing and listening to each other's needs is vital for a loving and committed relationship.

Taking responsibility in a relationship means acknowledging that each partner is accountable for their own role in creating, sustaining or breaking down the relationship. When both partners have an attitude of accountability, then it reflects a couple committed to supporting each other for the wellbeing of their relationship.

THE FOUR HORSEMEN OF THE APOCALYPSE

A couple who are committed to, and take responsibility for their roles in the relationship, also ensure that the way they interact with each other is predominantly positive and constructive. Conversely, researchers have shown that they could predict the end of a relationship when a couple's predominant styles of communication included what they call the *Four Horsemen of the Apocalypse* (www.gottman.com):

* Criticism
* Contempt
* Defensiveness
* Stonewalling

When you criticise your partner, you are attacking their person ("you're always late!") where as complaining is about an issue ("I was scared when you didn't phone me as we had planned"). When you or your partner continually criticise one another then it feels like a sustained personal attack and the feeling of hurt and rejection could spiral in to the other more severe negative interactions — or Horsemen.

Having contempt for your partner is mocking, disregarding or demeaning him/her. It can be in the form of body language, such as eye-rolling or sighing, with the effect of causing your partner to feel worthless. This behaviour is a single predictor of divorce and needs to be eliminated urgently if the relationship is to be restored.

Defensiveness is probably a response we have all used. In a rocky relationship, excuses are perceived by your partner that a request is not being taken seriously, and to make things worse, the defensiveness is turned into blame of the other. "Did you phone the Wrights this morning to say we wouldn't be able to come to dinner this evening?" "You know how busy I am, why didn't you do it?"

When one partner shuts him/herself down and no longer responds or listens to the other, he/she is stonewalling. It could be in the form of 'tuning out' or suddenly becoming very busy and therefore avoidant of the other when they are trying to communicate. Sometimes people simply ignore the other person or walk out the room. While many of us may have had occasion to 'stonewall' a person, when it is frequent or habitual it is likely to contribute to the termination of a relationship.

THE FOUR HORSEMEN

Criticism: Verbally attacking personality or character.
Contempt: Attacking your partner's sense of self with intention to insult or psychologically abuse him/her.
Defensiveness: Seeing yourself as the victim in attempt to ward off an attack, and there by shift the blame.
Stonewalling: Withdrawing from the relationship in at-

tempt to avoid conflict and convey distance, disapproval and separation.

ANTIDOTES TO THE FOUR HORSEMEN

If you notice you've been criticising your partner, try to use "I" instead of "you" when you need something to change. Instead of: "You are always late!", try "I feel nervous when you don't call and tell me you're running late". When you become aware that you have verbally abused or insulted your partner, in other words, showed contempt for him/her, take a moment to consider their positive attributes. What is working in the relationship? This may be a difficult process, but if your relationship is to survive and heal, then this is one of the most important negative interactions to eliminate. At an appropriate time, verbalise your appreciation of your partner. All human beings need to feel validated.

Not being defensive requires an attitude switch, where you decide to rather take responsibility for your behaviour. There are times when you are clearly in the wrong and being the 'victim' and blaming the other simply undermines you and your relationship. Accepting your partner's perspective is a show of commitment to your partner and strengthens the relationship.

Withdrawing or removing yourself physically or psychologically from your partner, or stonewalling, because you feel disempowered, will not help heal a rift in the relationship. It requires courage to admit you are unable to interact adequately. Consider taking a break by perhaps going for a walk, and then find a more constructive way of interacting with your partner.

Of course, your relationship may be at a point where you are not able to talk respectfully with each other. In this case, if you haven't decided to go your separate ways, I would strongly advise making an appointment with a relationship counsellor.

When Jenny and Steve consulted me regarding their marriage, it was clear that they were in a very difficult space. Jenny was angry and tended to glare at Steve, whilst Steve's clenched jaw and resentful attitude spoke volumes about his feelings towards Jenny, as well as his having to attend this counselling session.

"You are our last resort," Jenny said to me. "If we don't fix this, our relationship is over." From where I was sitting, this relationship was in big trouble. I asked Jenny to tell me more about what was happening and why she felt their relationship had reached breaking-point. She described how she felt alone and unappreciated, that Steve expected her to take full responsibility for running the home, caring for the children and holding down a full-time job.

As she described her side of the story, I noticed Steve's resigned expression, as if to say, "here we go again, the same old complaint".

"Steve," I asked, "what is your take on why your relationship has got to this point?" I waited a few moments while he gathered his thoughts and began tentatively, "we have kinda drifted apart... I don't feel I can put a foot right... and I'm tired of trying to second-guess what Jenny wants."

"I don't think you love me anymore, Steve. You're right. We have drifted apart..." and then Jenny's angry face collapsed and tears started to fall.

Steve looked uncomfortable but had the courage to speak up. "This is the kind of pattern – we get angry with each other, tears are shed, but we can't seem to build ourselves back up again. It's as if there's no energy left to try anymore."

Jenny described how she grew up in a family where her father was an alcoholic and struggled to keep a job. Her mother did her best to work and provide for Jenny and her two siblings, but life was tough financially. As Jenny grew older, she resented the fact that her mother didn't leave her father who was abusive to her and the children. Jenny swore to herself that she would never live in poverty again, nor be treated by her husband in the way her father treated her mother.

Steve grew up in a fairly stable family. He and his brother got on well. His parents modelled a couple that were independent and capable, but not warm and affectionate with each other. The family motto was "be self-sufficient". Sharing one's feelings did not come readily to Steve or his family, so he learned to suppress them. He was a proficient company manager of a small team of employees and had a reputation for being a 'black and white' thinker.

After several sessions, steps were put in place to help Steve and Jenny feel emotionally safe to express their needs. They learned that where Jenny tended to be over-responsible and keep a tight rein on the family finances and home life, this was coming from a place of anxiety, of "not being enough" and "not having enough". In doing this, part of her was longing for Steve to acknowledge and recognise that she was indeed "enough". She wasn't, unfortunately, able to articulate this and instead became frustrated and angry that Steve displayed little empathy for her. Jenny was not able to 'responsibly' express how she felt and what her needs were. She expected Steve to just 'know'.

Steve, coming from his background of "self-sufficiency", was initially attracted to Jenny because she had similar values and aspirations. Not being able to see why Jenny was unhappy, or express his own needs adequately, Steve simply felt attacked. He reacted by responding angrily or shutting down. Both understood that their use of some of the Four Horsemen communication styles came from a place of feeling disempowered. They recognised how destructive these tactics were for the relationship.

In learning to express their needs in an emotionally safe environment, Steve and Jenny realised the importance of taking responsibility for verbalising what they needed from each other, rather than expecting the other to guess what they required. Jenny stopped demanding Steve continually affirm her. In fact, she didn't need to any more as Steve was more attentive towards her around the house. At Jenny's request, Steve began to help with managing the finances. He also experienced the gratifying feeling of being needed and valued by Jenny and the children.

In our relationship house analogy, couples who take responsibility for effectively articulating their needs within a committed relationship are symbolised by strong and reliable, load-bearing walls. Such a relationship has the following characteristics:

* A desire to share time with each other.

* Sharing important decision-making.

* Sharing financial decisions, including the signing of contracts.

* Sharing future plans.

* Spending holiday time together.

* Considering each other in daily activities

EXERCISE

Consider where you may fall short in the areas of responsibility and commitment within the relationship. Do you use some, or all, of the Four Horsemen of the Apocalypse when communicating? What do you think you could change, or which behaviours would you suggest need replacing?

Going Deeper

INTROVERT

EXTROVERT

Part of being responsible and accountable is the ability to be self-aware. Being aware of our personality make-up, our attributes and weaknesses, and having clear boundaries in terms of our norms and values, makes taking responsibility and being accountable within a relationship much less complex. At the very least, one can navigate tricky times much more easily.

Here's a good example. I'm sure there are times when you wonder how it is that your partner can behave so differently from you in a given set of circumstances. For example, he says: "Let's invite people for drinks and dinner. Will be great to see Jack and Sal again. And let's also invite John and his girlfriend." She says: We have been out twice this week, already. Please! Let's have a quiet evening at home." He says: "You seldom seem to want to socialise." She says to herself: "You seem to thrive on other people's company."

Knowing each other's differing personality types gives one a better foundation for negotiation.

In this example, we have two sharply differing personalities – he is more **extrovert** and she more **introvert**.

Carl Jung described personality types as falling on the spectrum of introvert-extrovert. There is no absolute introvert or extrovert, but rather a tendency towards one or the other. The defining element that characterises someone as being more introvert or more extrovert seems to be one's energy levels. Those with an abundance of energy tend to be extroverts. The reverse is true for introverts.

In many cases, people fall somewhere in between depending on the circumstances. These people are described as ambiverts. Jacob Shriar expands on the theory in his *Key Differences Between Introverts and Extroverts:*

* They recharge differently: Introverts prefer to recharge after a social event on their own. After gathering and consolidating their depleted energy levels, they will be able to socialise once more. Extroverts thrive on social interaction. They feel energised in social interactions.

* They connect differently: Introverts tend to connect better on a one-to-one basis, whereas extroverts are happy in group settings.

* They have different levels of relationships: Introverts tend to have fewer friends but deeper relationships, whilst extroverts may have many friends with less depth of relationship.

* Communication is different: Introverts tend to listen more, and extroverts tend to talk more.

* They deal differently with change: Introverts tend to enjoy stability and structure so may not enjoy change as much as extroverts, who could find themselves energised by change.

* Different levels of focus: Introverts need quiet and will be distracted by noise; they are more reflective and introspective. Extroverts are happily and easily distracted, ready to share and chat about things.

When a couple understands that each has an inherently different personality and that their partner is not necessarily being resistant, but is rather expressing themselves differently as they interact with the world, they are more willing to accommodate each other's quirks.

Chapter 6

THE WINDOWS: TRANSPARENCY

We cultivate love when we
allow our most vulnerable and
powerful selves to be deeply
seen and known.
— Brené Brown

In our super-connected world where more and more information is laid bare on social media, where transparency is demanded from politicians, service-providers, food labels, you name it, expecting consistent transparency in our intimate relationships is not necessarily that easy or straightforward.

Transparency is scary. It means revealing ourselves — how we feel and what our needs are — and thus opening ourselves to criticism or rejection.

This can be threatening for some partners, particularly where there have been hurtful past experiences.

The truth is, without transparency we find ourselves less connected and lonelier within our relationship. But being open and transparent allows us to connect on a much deeper level. This is the experience of intimacy (in-to-me-see). The more we're able to be vulnerable and talk about sensitive subjects, to allow our partner to truly 'see' us, the more authentic our relationship. It requires that both partners commit to honouring the trust they expect of each other.

Building on the analogy of the house-windows, we are constantly observing our partners, making assessments and judging them. We use all our senses in a constant feedback loop to assess our partner's non-verbal cues such as hunched shoulders, abrupt speech, or subtle signals such as the size of the pupil and the muscles around the eye, to build a picture of their mood.

How are you feeling? Are you happy? Sad? Contented? Can you see that I'm hurt? What if you notice how angry I really am? Is it 'safe' for me to chat with you, or am I going to be ignored, criticised or judged? When all is said and done, we want and need to 'see' and 'be seen' by each other. Being transparent requires that there be congruency between your non-verbal and verbal communication, allowing your partner to truly understand how you are feeling – rather than having them try to interpret mixed signals.

An inability to be transparent suggests that there is a lack of trust between you and your partner. If you or your partner has been hurt before, whether in your present relationship, a previous relationship, or even as a child, then you will probably have a well-defined 'wall' of protection around you. While this helps to protect you from further hurt, ironically it may prevent you from enjoying a deeply meaningful relationship with your beloved.

If you have experienced hurt and trauma resulting in difficulty being completely open and transparent, and you find it difficult to enjoy a loving and connected relationship, consider seeing a relationship expert. You and your partner will benefit from the experience.

In the previous chapter, Jenny and Steve learned how to safely express their needs and expectations. Their interactions with each other became more transparent as they allowed themselves to be vulnerable. As a result, the couple enjoyed a deeper, warmer connection with each other. They commented that the road had been rocky at times, but it was a journey they believed had brought them together in the first place. Now much wiser for the experience, they felt they were living a truly authentic relationship.

Together with your partner, reveal one subject that you haven't revealed before. Remember this process requires practice – the more you do this in an emotionally safe way – the more you will feel comfortable being transparent with each other.

Refresh your memories about each other's values and your combined mission statement. Is there anything in these exercises where you feel you could be more transparent? Share this now with your partner.

Going Deeper

This above all: to thine own self
be true, And it must follow, as
the night the day, Thou canst not
then be false to any man.
— Polonius in Shakespeare's
Hamlet

If we were consistently true to ourselves then life would probably be a little less complicated. In a world that is so socially prescribed, that's a big ask. There is often an internal battle inside ourselves where we are weighing up the pros and cons of behaving (i) according to social norms and cultural values and (ii) from a place we instinctively know is authentic behaviour coming from who we 'really' are. The one may have diametrically different outcomes from the other, but the one is dictated by social conditioning and the other is inspired by one's heart.

Finding our authentic voice while also being mindful of social norms requires balance that is sometimes a challenge. There is no doubt that when we live more connected to what Martha Beck describes as our 'essential self' rather than allow ourselves to be dominated by our 'social self', our lives take on a vibrant quality of energy and purpose.

Discovering your 'essential self' usually requires some work and I would highly recommend consulting with a psychologist, life coach or other professional who will help you on this worthwhile journey of self-discovery. I also encourage you to read Martha Beck's books (see References & Resources).

Knowing yourself and being comfortably transparent with your partner is a place and space we all aspire towards. This is where we can describe our relationship as intimate and connected.

Working towards self-knowledge is a life-long process and being in relationship is one of the best, and often most uncomfortable (!) opportunities to move us along in this process. Our partners will consistently mirror aspects about ourselves that, if we're open and available, we'll acknowledge and learn a valuable lesson.

Chapter 7

Between right thinking and
wrong thinking there is a field.
I will meet you there.
— Rumi

Trust is choosing to risk making
something you value vulnerable
to another person's actions.
— Charles Feltman

The subject of emotional safety is a common theme throughout this book. It is such an important subject that one could say the health of your relationship is either built up on or broken down to the extent that you feel emotionally safe with your partner.

Emotional safety is about trust. If all the other aspects discussed in earlier chapters – clear values, good communication skills, effective boundaries, taking responsibility for the relationship, commitment and transparency – are in place and working, then the 'roof' of your relationship house represents the safety and protection you feel within a lovingly maintained relationship.

When Jenny and Steve began their consultations with me, they felt extremely disconnected from each other. They were unable to effectively communicate their needs and concerns with the result that Jenny's feelings of being unheard and unappreciated escalated into anger towards Steve. Steve, meanwhile, felt that Jenny was being unreasonable and emotional. He had no idea how to approach Jenny, so he simply withdrew and effectively stonewalled her.

What was urgently needed was that all-important conversation where they simply let their defences down and began a heart-to-heart conversation about their situation.

In the safety of my office, Jenny and Steve were able to start a meaningful conversation about their struggles, fears and desires. Guiding the couple to open themselves up to each other – where each had an opportunity to say what was on their mind, and where the other carefully listened without judging – there came a special moment when the couple realised that the defensive walls which were meant to protect their hurt feelings, were in fact a barrier to a meaningful connection with each other.

They learned that being vulnerable with each other need not be something to feel ashamed or fearful of. They realised for example, Jenny's feeling of not being good enough; and Steve's feeling of being ashamed that he wasn't being an effective husband and able to 'fix' her feelings, were honest feelings that would be treated with respect and kindness. Expressing their vulnerabilities within an atmosphere of emotional safety, allowed them to share and connect on a much deeper level, including the rekindling of a much-improved sex-life!

Emotional safety is a two-way process. It is an experience of being vulnerable with your partner and knowing at the same time your vulnerability is being supported and respected. It's a heartfelt ability of both partners to share their deepest thoughts, fears, inadequacies and not to be judged for expressing these. As the Research Sociologist, Brené Brown, reminds us: "Vulnerability is the birthplace of love, belonging, joy, courage, empathy, accountability, and authenticity."

In the stress of daily life, we may overlook the need for our partner to feel safe and connected. When we feel neglected or attacked for long enough, or deeply enough, it can escalate to the point where a couple feels incapable of making bids for connection.

The relationship becomes paralysed. Ideally, before it reaches this point, couples who are more in tune with each other recognise that their relationship is under strain: they're snapping at each other, avoiding each other, feeling tired and frustrated or experiencing similar signals. No matter how tired and frustrated you may feel, try to take a few minutes (or more) to reach out to your partner. The solution may not be immediately apparent but the simple gesture of spending some quality time truly listening to each other ensures a space of emotional safety.

EXERCISE

Do you feel you are able to (i) give and (ii) receive emotional safety with your partner? Provide examples. Where do you think you might improve? How does your partner feel about your answers?

Going Deeper

Returning to Rumi's quotation "Between right thinking and wrong thinking there is a field. I will meet you there," I believe 'the field' is a wonderful analogy for common ground.

Common ground is a space where two people can meet and find matters of common interest or agreement. It is also a place where, with intention, they can meet in neutrality. This neutral space is also one that is open for possibility. The experience of the meeting in this 'field' can come as a relief to conflicting couples. They discover that when they release their defended positions, positions usually established from a place of fear, they enjoy the freedom of meeting each other without the threat of judgment or criticism. Now there are new beginnings, new understandings and new possibilities.

It takes enormous presence of mind for partners to rise above the emotional drama of the moment and build a bridge of trust back to each other. The art of 'bridge building' takes practice. It is an exercise used extensively in Imago Therapy (see Reference & Resources), teaching couples to expertly listen and understand what their partner's experience of a situation is, without judging. The outcome of this exercise is indeed a meeting in a field of possibility where a bridge of trust exists, and common ground is firmly established.

The dilemma, and also the aspiration for all of us, whether single or in relationship, is the need for 'safety'. We look for financial, physical, mental, social and emotional safety. Interestingly, research detailed at *stephenporges.com* shows that it is a biological reality that is hard-wired to instinctively establish whether that 'other' is 'safe', and this instinct extends to all mammals. In their case, the focus is on physical protection of others as a survival mechanism. We humans also have this survival mechanism and it is also applied to social and emotional safety, the mainstay of which are our intimate relationships.

Consider how we instinctively and continuously 'read' whether our partner is in a good mood or whether there is sadness or anger or something troubling him or her. We could say we are judging whether it is momentarily 'safe' to interact with our partner.

For example, can I trust my partner to hear my problem without judgment? If my partner cannot be trusted, then I am unlikely to share intimate or personal information. I will probably take a defensive or protective position in the relationship. Conversely, where partners feel confident and trusting of their partners, they experience emotional safety. There is an openness, a transparency, between partners that usually comes from personal growth and maturity, resulting in a truly authentic and connected relationship.

Chapter 8

PULLING IT ALL TOGETHER:

MAKING OUR HOUSE A HOME

Your relationship house reflects the quality and careful attention you have given to your relationship. A lick of paint here, replacing light-bulbs there, fixing a leaking tap, replacing a tile, etc. All of this is evidence of the commitment you have for maintaining your house. It's common sense that the more you care for and maintain it, rather than taking it for granted or neglecting it, the better it will serve you, your partner and family.

Fixing and maintaining is very important for a well-functioning house. What, though, would make it an even warmer, inviting and safe home?

Whilst I have referred to physical structures such as the floor, windows, walls and so on as metaphors for skills to repair or improve your relationship, there are even more nuanced activities that can enhance your house, make it feel like a 'home' and in this way experience a deeper connection with your beloved.

For example, I love having flowers in my lounge – for me it suggests that no matter how simply decorated the home, bringing a little nature into the house is bringing appreciation, life and energy into the living space. It is an expression of fulfilment and nurturing that I wish to give and share with my beloved. For some, having a comfortable dining area where food, conversation and sharing is an important expression of a warm home. Your creativity is limitless. A colourful scatter cushion, warm-toned paint on the walls, pretty lighting, comfortable chairs, candles, thoughtfully prepared food and drink, and so on, all lends to an ambiance of togetherness and enjoyment.

There may be other areas of one's house that may be significant for you or your partner. What are these for you?

For example, the bedroom. Is your bedroom a safe space for love and intimacy? For healing sleep too? You've begun communicating openly and honestly with each other, paying attention to each other's love languages. What do you believe would improve this important space? This may be a mutual decision to move the TV to another room. What is your understanding of the use of cellphones or other communication devices in the bedroom? When you are together in the bedroom, are you able to really hear each other's needs, meet each other on a deeply emotional as well as physical level? This is a space where a couple can truly meet each other in an atmosphere of trust and emotional safety.

In order for your relationship to thrive and taking into account all the skills and life experiences achieved to date, the 'glue' that sustains and nurtures it, in my opinion, is the ability to be fully present with each other. Another way of saying this is: show up, no matter what. Of course, this is easier said than done in highly emotionally charged situations, but there is always the opportunity for learning about the effectiveness of your inner resources and building an even stronger relationship. Be messy, be vulnerable, but show up. You owe it to yourself and your relationship will benefit hugely.

CIRCUMSTANCES CHANGE: PREPARE TO ADAPT

One thing we've all had to come to terms with in the 21st Century is that while we have the ability to put plans into place and have many skills and resources at our disposal to have better control over our lives, life tends to throw us curved balls to test all our theories and experiences. Change is inevitable.

I have a friend whose husband has recently retired. There are new dynamics at play now that her hubby spends more time at home. Mischa was up until this time used to her own 'space' around the house. Anticipating possible difficulties in adjusting to being around and 'under Mischa's feet', Bob decided to turn his hand to an old past-time, woodwork. He is busy making a 'den' for himself. When that's finished, he is making a patio – something Mischa has wanted for a long time. He will also play golf more frequently.

The couple have found constructive ways to be together without too much infringement on their boundaries. In other words, they've found ways to accommodate each other's need for space, yet be together in a more relaxed phase of their lives. They were fortunate enough to anticipate an important (and predictable) change in their lives which they managed well.

This is an example of a couple who have a good connection. They have learned the necessary skills to ensure that their relationship is well-maintained so when changes occur they are able to adapt to a new rhythm without losing the core purpose and meaning of their relationship.

What happens when life 'as we knew it' is changed irrevocably? There are countless examples of where life-changing circumstances have resulted in a failed relationship. In the case of death, the loss of a relationship is the result. A sick child, financial ruin, war, emigration and infidelities are other examples.

There is no 'golden rule' for handling severe change that I know of. There are various options to consider, however. You will figure out what makes sense for your particular circumstances as you go along. In the meantime, here are some considerations:

* Talk to someone. Start with your beloved or, if that's not possible, then approach or be open to hearing from others who have been in a similar position to gain insight. While you may instinctively withdraw from life as you take stock of your situation, being in touch with a trustworthy person who can support you during this difficult time is important for your recovery from this shock.

* Accept that your life will have chaotic moments. Find ways to nurture yourself as you take time to grieve the loss of what was. It really is okay to be vulnerable.

* Remind yourself what your goals were for your relationship. These may have changed somewhat, but if you're still committed to being with each other, then it may be time to re-evaluate these goals. Communicating authentically about your needs will help your relationship find a new 'normal'.

A relationship that is built on a solid foundation, where both parties have the clear intention of remaining 100% invested, allows couples to find ways of adapting to life's curved balls—big or small.

CONCLUSION

LAST BUT NOT LEAST

This book has been about practical solutions to every day relationship problems, but the truth is that relationships are as unique as the individuals within them. Similarly, relationships grow and evolve with time and life experience. There are no 'rules' but there are expectations built up on social, cultural and personal norms which help guide us towards common objectives.

Having worked through the chapters of this book it should be apparent that your relationship house will be a manifestation of how much attention you have paid to the maintenance and wellbeing of your unique relationship.

FINAL EXERCISE

If you did a health check as suggested at the beginning of the book, now would be a good time to do another rating of the health of your relationship. Hopefully it has substantially improved. Consider writing in your journal what exercises or insights worked for you. In terms of 'house maintenance' what do you feel you and your partner need to do in order to sustain the changes you made? Your suggestions could be incorporated in your earlier mission statement.

IN SUMMARY

Phillip C. McGraw says: "In relationships, just as in every other aspect of life, the spirit and attitude with which you do things is at least as important as your actual actions... To start the reconnection process with your partner, you must passionately adopt the proper spirit (attitude)". If you have read and worked through this book, your attitude and intention to make the necessary changes will have already begun to reignite your relationship. Congratulations!

REFERENCES

Martha Beck, *www.marthabeck.com*

Dr Eric Berne, M.D. *www.ericberne.com/transactional analysis*

Dr Brené Brown, *www.brenebrown.com*

Gary Chapman, *Five Languages of Love* (1995)

Dr John Demartini , *www.demartini.com*

Emerson Eggerichs, *Love & Respect: The Love She Most Desires; The Respect He Desperately Needs*

Freepik. 2019. House vector created by freepik - *www.freepik.com/free-vector/houses-collection_791498.htm*

Shirley P Glass, *Not "Just Friends": Rebuilding Trust and Recovering Your Sanity After Infidelity*

Dr John Gottman, *Gottman's 4 Four Horses Horsemen of the Apocalypse, www.gottman.com*

Imago Therapy, *www.imagotherapy.co.za*

Phillip C. McGraw, *Relationship Rescue* (2000)

Dr S Karpman, *DramaTriangle, www.karpmandrama-triangle.com*

Judy Klipin, *Lessons for The Adult Child (2010), www.judyklipin.com*

Patricia Love & Steven Stosny, *Why Women Talk and Men Walk – How to Improve Your Relationship Without Discussing It* (2007)

Esther Perel, *The State of Affairs: Rethinking Infidelity*

Senge, PM, Klieiner, A., Roberts, C., *The Fifth Discipline Field book: Strategies and Tools*

Ross, RB, and Smith, BJ, *Strategies and Tools for Building a Learning Organization* (1994)

Jacob Shriar, *www.officevibe.com/blog/differences-introverts-extroverts*

RESOURCES

Life Line Southern Africa: tel. +27 11 715 2000

Relationship Counselling, RSA
www.psychotherapy.co.za
www.safamily.co.za/counselling
www.therapist-directory.co.za